Rapunzel's Braid

Rapunzel's Braid

Beau Boudreaux

Five Oaks Press
FIVE-OAKS-PRESS.COM

Other works by Beau Boudreaux:

Significant Other
Running Red, Running Redder

Copyright ©2016 Beau Boudreaux
All rights reserved. First print edition.

Five Oaks Press
Newburgh, NY 12550
five-oaks-press.com
editor@five-oaks-press.com

ISBN: 978-1-944355-20-3

Cover & Book Design: Lynn Houston

Printed in the United States of America

ACKNOWLEDGMENTS

The Ambriel Revolution: "For Granted," "The Moon Is Troubling"
Belle Reve Literary Journal: "Camille," "Coupon," "Love Poem"
Big River Poetry Review: "Velleity"
The Coachella Review: "Whitefish Bay"
Colours Journal: "Bound" "Peachtree Roads"
Duende: "Nursing"
East Jasmine Review: "Junior Year"
Edwin E. Smith's Quarterly Magazine: "Michael," "Smoke," "Swan"
Ellipses…Literature and Art: "Saison D'Ecrivisses"
Fox Cry Review: "Lakeview Drive," "New Year's Eve"
Foxing Quarterly: "Forgotten Garden"
Four Chambers Press: "Everywhere At Once"
Iron Gall Press: "Blossoming Magnolia"
Leveler: "Rapture"
Lines + Stars: "South Shore Harbor"
Louisiana Literature: "Audubon Golf Course," "Harry's Ace Hardware," "Soft Shell Crabs," and "Shorewood"
Mason's Road Literary Journal: "Swings"
Mandela Journal: "Miles," "Newborn Son"
Marathon Literary Review: "Accidents Happen" and "My Maid Takes Her Shoes Off"
Mixitini Matrix: "Monday"
94 Creations: "Attic"
Pea River Journal: "Proposal"
Poetry Quarterly: "Gabriel Falls Into A Shallow Pool of Disgrace" and "Moment of Weakness"
Rappahannock Review: "You Can Touch Me"
Rose Red Review: "Blue Gardenia"
Silhouette Press: "Avocado"

The Paddle Wheeler: "Ben Franklin Senior High, 1993," "Gambling," and "Sonny"
The Rusty Nail: "Freeman School." "Punting"
Subliminal Interiors Literary Arts Magazine: "Courtship"
Tincture Journal: "Carnival"
Torrid Literature: "You Are Not Here Yet"
VAYVAVYA: "Divorcé, Dispirited"

Many thanks to the editors who selected poems to be included in their anthologies: Mississippi River Poetry Anthology 2015, Reckless Writing Poetry Anthology 2013.

For Heather

CONTENTS

I.

Soft Shell Crabs	7
Audubon Golf Course	8
Junior Year	9
Swings	10
Ben Franklin Senior High, 1993	11
Punting	12
Spillway	13
Gambling	14
Forgotten Garden	15
Blue Gardenia	16
L'heure de l'apéritif	17
Peachtree Roads	18
Blossoming Magnolia	19
You Can Touch Me	20
Rapture	21
Swan	22
South Shore Harbor	23
Smoke	24
Miles	25
New Year's Eve	26
Love Poem	27

II.

Everywhere At Once	31
Streets of Mid-City	32
Saison D'Ecrivisses	33
Camille	34
Bound	35
Freeman School	36
Velleity	37
Coupon	38
Accidents Happen	39
Undone	40

Shorewood	41
Whitefish Bay	43
Michael	44
Sonny	45
Gabriel Falls Into A Shallow Pool Of Disgrace	46
Lakeview Drive	47
Mother of the Bride	48
Failing On One Knee	49

III.

For Granted	53
The Moon Is Troubling	54
Proposal	55
Carnival	56
Attic	57
Harry's Ace Hardware	58
Dizzy Dean Baseball	59
My Maid Takes Her Shoes Off	60
Dawn Till Dusk	61
Moment of Weakness	62
Divorcé, Dispirited	63
Nursing	64
Newborn Son	65
Toddler	66
Avocado	67
Monday	68

I

Soft Shell Crabs

Show a little early this season
before the full moon in May

like pulling gold bracelets
from their well—

four and half inches are prime
just four called hotels

and at the street market
they run out early

faster than the hot tamales
and speckled trout

a fever, frenzy for the fragile
crusts that molt a delicacy

sizzling in a wrought iron pan.

Audubon Golf Course

Dusk, popping a top water lure—
chrome propeller and treble hooks

not a trace of another person
the pond's surface like plates of glass

ripples when a dragonfly lands—
I've not had a strike. Patience sets

in and I enjoy long casts along the shoreline
wonder if I'm using the right lure

or am at the spot where Michael tore
them up last evening, largemouth bass swim

less than ten minutes from my doorstep
in a posted lagoon daytime, turned paradise by twilight.

Junior Year

The morning streetcar ride
up St. Charles

meet Jason at the front of Audubon Park
walk to the grocery store

for Colt 45 malt liquor
and pass the zoo to the Mississippi

watching barges float by
drinking our 40 ounces

as old men set their hooks
into catfish

skipping bottle caps
down to the Gulf of Mexico.

Swings

There was a beat up ice chest, ice cubes covered
in Florida Water soaking a cloth rag

for the back of the neck
or to pat your face.

I was nine and barely could glove the ball.
Practice began in early June, Coach Lupo

a sultan with a taped wood fungo bat—
stained jockey t-shirt and round gut

had a deal with the weather, brief afternoon showers
would stop at three for practice,

for two hours I learned
to focus, stay down on grounders,

toss them to first, side-arm to second
automatic, safe wearing a cup that he would check

with a tap of his bat before fungo, before we could take
the field—a reminder for cover, protection

how skin encases the fruit.

Ben Franklin Senior High, 1993

Each scrimmage took a yellow bus ride
to the Butterfly, a mile or so of grass

kissing the Mississippi—
coach only gave water as a reward

helmet and pads in August heat
dripping sweat

we drilled, took knees to rest
became lean, made teammates

running a wing-T formation, fooling
a few teams with our option

always playing their homecomings
and our own on the opponent's field.

Punting

The way a football spins
spiraling from the side of my foot

like a car tire
catching a long patch of ice

for once during a game
pinning the opponent sixty yards

down the field
as boys smoke under

the stands, cheerleaders cheer
through a starry night in Gramercy…

my Catholic school girlfriend
seduces a close buddy in the bleachers

of awe as I kick the ball—

like nothing—
my touchdown called back

for a hold—
caught interception ruled out of bounds.

Spillway

The pregnant Mississippi
eye-levels the levee

Morganza gates and Bonnet Carre bays
wide open—

barges ominous, appear larger
we're blessed

peeling crawfish, sip cans of Dixie
sunsets on Memorial day—

frisbees, kites, bicycles
Harley-Davidsons

call, echo
as the ferries flow

men cast for catfish
lovers on wood benches

wonder why I'm not up here
more often—

freeloading this outdoor cinema
smiling at good women

with their barbecue chicken
freed from their coops.

Gambling

Sunday's Times-Picayune
reported an old friend
jumped into the Mississippi

from a casino boat after midnight—
he was all-smiles, ready for a laugh
and from a good family…

I pictured a big loss at the tables
drove him over the rail,
not a stunt or dare

the river would have been a shock
especially if he'd been drinking
and the current deep and deadly—

but he was recovered
unclear if by Coast Guard
or if he swam to shore.

Forgotten Garden

Two blocks from Audubon
her driveway overgrown

with jasmine and ficus
scraping against your car

leads to a side path, stone foot walk
beyond her cement garage

underneath her private garden
camellias and pecan trees

form a giant umbrella
sun glints through,

sprays on a trim lawn
her granite white bench

where fairies gather
for a syrup whiskey sour

I whack a wiffle ball
with a yellow bat into the bushes

erupting mud daubers
wings like exclamation points

that sting bejeezus
from my arm's nectar.

Blue Gardenia

Bulbs of opaque light ebb
a shot of bourbon

hush of late evening, electric murmur
couples in clouds of smoke,

whispers hush her on stage
microphone an altar, divining rod

tall men lean against the mahogany bar
we pause for an unguarded moment

she begins her part, sway the crowd
brush back her sienna-brown locks

a camel chemise, chamois voice
courses us downstream for the evening.

L'heure de l'apéritif

She in Chardonnay dress
empties her glass
sapphire necklace catches
chandelier light—golden haired
chignon commands the room.

Peachtree Roads

This heat, city with its concentric circles
form a brief spell, an uprising golden spiral

honey, bring this garland home from the gorge
bring me health, woman in blonde bun

your carriage arrives, I shift
submissive, the stones stack the wall

balcony opens up to sway of sycamore
a quick, brief afternoon

shower—lips ripe to kiss, skin shade of pink
like watermelons stacked and sliced

in pick-up beds on old Elysian Fields.

Blossoming Magnolia

I can't determine beauty

strands everywhere—
bedroom pillows, tiles of the bathroom floor,

my mouth...
blinded by her iris, chimes of her voice

like a newfound instrument, orphic whistle in the trees
a part wants out of this

entire seduction
find again the old winding path back to the marina

where I can be alone again
not longing, not pitiful...

I don't know what to think
so I think everything

alarmed, deeply uncertain
her conception of self and experience

bone by bone.

You Can Touch Me

if you want, your wish
the lemon grove and lime trees

are heavy, giving and the rain
comes only in late afternoon

I can let my hair down
with a shake and look more

appetizing, a plate of oysters
on the half-shell, pâté with sliced

pears—the oriental rug aired in
sunshine, its worn diamond design—

pool balls racked on felt
please, honey take the cue.

Rapture

This loosening fall air
button unbuttons

unzip, zip of her
sweater perhaps opens

up a sliver
of a sunshot horizon

decision to pull
or let down her hair

key lime pie
sweet tea

tugs the leash
towards her jasmine scent

at the turn of the corner
ball over the fence.

Swan

Now as I glide above
the current accepts my wing

for what is my hollow December
proposal, ghost on my knee

seeks surcease, seeks some
shelter and yes I am no longer

the drag from your cigarette
burn through tobacco like straw—

I've found your harbor
chain wrenched from the ball

give nothing to have you
back—take a hand

mirror for the first time, twist—
your peculiar attraction

my beak with jagged teeth
dabbling your shoulder

between us, who could never be alone?
I claim victory, my grace Leda

Queen of Sparta tonight
maybe, late, a clutch in a few weeks…

I will not come again
in this form.

South Shore Harbor

Waves lick the long shore
bobbing skiffs moored in the marina

raise their sails like flaps
of envelopes waiting for their messages

as if cold, or sick with fever
her voice shook when I touched her arm

her tipped globe of Bordeaux
waving around my face a violet perfume

when I looked her in the eye
she turned away to address the commodore.

Smoke

I'm jealous of the man
who polishes a thick filet

rises from the linen table
for a smoke.

I've been sniffing my sweater
as Moms do in high school…

this year laws stormed all
blew out the knock-knock bar

where you could toke
up conversation

now, indoors it's like grandma's
jasmine miasma as you round a corner

seeking the intimate movie scene
on horseback, by the beach

this romantic carrying a box
of matches

though there's no one, really
left to light.

Miles

I jogged the shoulder of a service road
in Hattiesburg steaming summer

stopped short to collect empty cigarette packs
printed on the side five Marlboro miles

that I would rip off and stuff in my sock—
sometimes on good days I'd get close to fifty

miles from drivers who'd roll their windows
down and toss their empty trash—

like plucking pennies from a fountain

saving ten thousand
for an argyle Dopp kit from Philip Morris

that has endured many, many more miles
across states and overseas.

New Year's Eve

I woke early
read the Times

enjoyed
resolutions—weight

loss, clearing clutter, yoga—
Doonesbury, and Scorpio horoscope.

Drove to the market bought
lemons for oysters, crabmeat

smoked salmon, a bottle of decent champagne...

thought about
black tie affairs

grabbing the nearest woman
at midnight and dipping her with passion.

I sat in my office at home
a light rain

the dog in his bed
worried about the fireworks.

Love Poem

For the first time
I am in love with no one.

No phone calls, texts
late night or early morning doorbell

I read late, sleep and dream
choose to not remember…

lost like a runner
not knowing the distance, the course

capsized in the depths of the Pacfiic
treading water

and I drive sylvan streets slowly
listening to college radio

feed and take the beagle around
nod to the neighborhood…

a teen-age girl in twilight
toes in the lake at the edge of the pier.

II

Everywhere At Once

Into the library,
under oaks sheltering rain

Florian Larouse performs
classical guitar

attent while his hands
work the frets like delicate pistons

Prelude, Allemande, Courante

these strings endorsed
filmed and archived

by the studio console
Florian returns for an encore

Sarabande, Bouree, Gigue

we're high on a suspension bridge
far below ferry boats pass.

Streets of Mid-City

Saturday night after Jazz Fest
Coco Robicheaux strums guitar on the patio

lit up with cheap lights, couples pull out a sofa
in the backyard tap another keg of Abita Amber

a guy shucks oysters from burlap sacks for tips—
lemons, horseradish, on the half shell

craving for seafood during this BP oil spill ban—
tourists along the house's balustrade,

inside on satellite a prizefight,
and we're boiling more crawfish—

college students in bun huggers, cut-off tees, hustle raffle tickets,
a pirate's in suit and cutlass,

musicians lounge without instruments
in late April humidity creeps in like a cat

early showers from the Gulf offer a southeast breeze
for the weekend buzz revelers teem side streets

it's all free like plucking a camellia from a neighbor's tree
stealing a bouquet from a cemetery.

Saison D'Ecrivisses

Crawfish harvest comes early this season
in south Louisiana—less than four bucks

a pound—on target to rival gas by summer—
the drive out to the lake

where shrimp are weighed on metal scales
you take a number and wait

filets of speckled trout caught this morning
on display with stuffed flounder and redfish

it's hard to pass on a dozen boiled crabs
to go along with a sack of live crawfish—

on the way home little claws tick
in the backseat destined for the ten gallon pot

newspaper lays out like red carpet on the backyard table
water boils Zatarain's seasoning sealing their fate.

Camille

A thunderstorm takes my power
a quick whip of a mistresses' gown

my mood
a sunken ship

what's written on the screen
stolen away

run from my memory
rinses paint from a brush…

wish I had a generator
thinking about what's in the freezer

venison, crawfish bisque,
Rocky Road.

Bound

And the voice which I heard from heaven spake unto me again, and said, go and take the little book which is open in the hand of the angel which standeth upon the sea and upon the earth.
—Revelation, X, vii

So I committed, signed for the long haul
made a list
waltzed into the library, searched

the stacks, hungry, like open credit in a supermarket
and their angels and saints
in hardcover no longer on Amazon

Millay, Campana, Symbolist poets
under each arm more weight than
my gym routine—Tristram Shandy...

checked out and bagged out for an entire term
and I felt loose, curious
and took the long way home

under a tunnel of oaks like overturned novels
down Napolean to the wharf—
tankers, the railway, commerce

deliberate pace of barges
a restless river, my trunk of books.
begging a read.

Freeman School

The middle of a humid summer
he had not made tenure

and as an employee of the university
I was sent to box his office

one window looked out over the quad
the married dorm with empty bicycle racks

his wooden desk and four steel shelves full
of journals, thin and thick—The Economist

he never spoke
nor smoked from his pipe collection

the more I packed
became a backyard pool

emptying—no more kids' splashing
barbecue, laughter.

Velleity

Fact—something happened
in the graduate workshop,
death off his chest
like a bird loose from its cage flew
desperately around at last to rest, a trembling

page, throat cracked on each word
our skiff lowered the mainsail
girls didn't toss their hair
professor buttoned his coat

silence—a brick tossed
in this room without a window
I never lost
a brother, an infant.

Heat from the furnace
past eight, snowfall
no pizza or dancing, his pitch
over the plate has gone by,

we went down looking
for that evening, clapped him on the back
looking both ways walking to the car.

Coupon

Instead of writing poetry
I'm printing out a 25% off
coupon from CVS

made a list, convinced
of sudden I need Gillette's Fusion razors
and the new cologne.

Pulling in late to beat traffic
forgot my hat, coat, list
but am too smart

at this hour
I should be fast asleep
and so should Karen

working the cash register,
asks for my card
not why a guy buys

Quilted Northern, Doritos Cool Ranch
a Mr. Goodbar, and a fifth of Jack
for his ride home.

Accidents Happen

It's my fault
due a ticket for once

fey sigh or protest,
dumb birds align the wire

streets slick, improper
lane change, no mean avenue

here, past midnight the bejeezus waiting
like a leg breaking, giving—

pinball spins into
its hole

standing in shame in rainfall
sitting on the curb done in

weep
alligator tears, a good sign

people after midnight sleeping
through this storm.

Undone

> *Do not forget to entertain strangers, for by so doing some people have entertained angels without knowing it.*
> —Hebrews 13:2

Seems the best idea
like loosening a sailboat from its mooring

slave to the waves
very temporary, free

senses acute
frantic pace quickens.

Open robe for morning
paper outside the front door

squeal of tires sudden
losing etiquette—clean shave,

turn signals, shoes unlaced
fist in face

music too loud, on repeat
boots kick the roof

phoning relatives,
old friends, strangers.

Shorewood

Bob cut my hair
in North Milwaukee

sleek dirty snow, biting breeze
I drove there

his mother died, left him a Tudor
on Downer

we bought racks of ribs half-priced
drank cheap champagne late into evenings

talked about the lure East—
fame, living in New York City—

Bob scheduled afternoon appointments,
my time free from graduate school,

he would bring me along
in a gold beat-up Benz

these older clients
women who lived in large stone estates where

he would do their hair in the kitchen
for the opera, symphony, charity ball

a hive
of gossip and cigarettes, Chardonnay–

children, especially husbands disappeared
he weaved with his hands

teasing their hair
nothing like locks

of those I dated, ponytails
thick caramel strands…

pop crops, curly cues
and pumped up pixies

heavy makeup, mascara
eyelashes, heady perfume

I sipped wine gazing at their art
while Bob banked praise, and goodbye kisses.

Whitefish Bay

Lucifer tattoos himself with scripture
every seven hundred years

ink fades like varnish on teak
his body of tropic—still smokes

as if on film for cancer
can't do him in…

industrial northern cities
strange locales, Milwaukee

west wind winds off the lake
engines rev

nod at our unticketed speedometers
lull in the snowstorm—

I ride these sleet streets, scarred for proof
a silver R/90/6 from the war

he rides a maroon Ducati
in December snow

heads north, pregnant wife
under the sky pitch black, an enormous bean bag

I motor south
the mile littered with leaves

in the headlight like sparkling Krugerrands
to my underground heated garage.

Michael

> *Will you be angry with us forever?*
> *Will your anger never cease?*
>   —Psalm 85:5

No, he does not dress in linen—
a more incandescent white

his eyes green fire
shoulders like knives

only loans the keys
to bliss…

what we thought a choir
climbed the ladder

turned to him playing with lyres—
piano with his rangy hands

guitar man donning a Stetson hat
snakeskin belt and boots

sounds to heal every man
no mercy

pity laid us down like pawns
on squares too black

and white for Earth.

Sonny

From the higher order
quiet, tallest of angels

lithe, ageless pitcher
like a white pelican

mitt, a worn leather fist—
I'm seven maybe eight

frightened standing on a strip
of lawn as he winds up

holds nothing back
delivers a strike that crimsons

my palm, pitch and catch
not a word or tear

from our same colored eyes
his only grandson—

sun beats down
white beans simmer on the stove.

Gabriel Falls Into A Shallow Pool Of Disgrace

For not obeying a command
exactly as given and remained

for a while outside
the heavenly Curtain…

like a teenager punished
for neglecting curfew

Gabriel made a minor escape
a scrape on the face of the Lord's

expectation—certainly being
inside the Curtain's privilege

a good thing like keys to your
home with internet paid

endowed, the one time sent
to his room without dinner

not knowing, unsure this is temporary,
ephemeral

that window of light
beneath the crack of the door.

Lakeview Drive

Maybe not the woman
but the music sends me—

electric streetcars.
I'm behind the wheel of a black sports car

the speed, runs through
like grain alcohol

like a wet kiss.

Jail
when it's not clear

why you're locked up—burden thrown
cape lost

blowing the Breathalyzer…

her eyes piercing
not sorry, fool—

more chalk
for the experience.

Mother of the Bride

Freight train rolls by
behind the levee

white wood chairs litter the lawn
Woody is marrying my friend Anne-Marie

sky a still blue
holds the old crescent, spray of stars

at the plantation guest house
I sweat in my Brooks Brothers

e.e. cummings read
by the matron of honor, cinema of smiles

champagne flutes
chatter around the enormous room

there's nothing—really
for me to compare

dancing with the bride's mom
as Sinatra flies to the moon.

Failing On One Knee

I've got this knee-jerk feeling again
        where I ride reckless,

bareback, a pony—
        wake in a cold sweat

phone her
        late morning reveille

impulse—buy a silver motorcycle
        instead of a solitaire

skid accident—
        what waits to happen

like a coiled snake, the bejeezus
        advice from a friend

take it easy—
        traipsing over the bridge he burns.

III

For Granted

Our routine, morning texts
long distance-phone call after work
weekend three hour drive…

her voice more familiar
than mine—bed for one now
sleeps two, letters to post

thank you letters for gifts…
there's still an invisible fence
around me, kind the dog can't jump

a full fall, leaves on side streets
and I hurl a divining rod straight down
at a mile from Audubon

hope she can find the well
these intricacies like a purse
of loose diamonds on black felt.

The Moon Is Troubling

He lost nothing but weight
with her–mornings brighter, sleep deeper

she's in the kitchen
bangs of wrought iron pans

egg white omelettes—swiss cheese,
mushroom, spinach

steam of chickory
wasting him in bed

her blonde hair twists on blue sheets
a homing pigeon

with a voice like chimes
nymph's body, sylph-like

so light
he trembles, she's winter chill

he's waiting on her each word
like the dog during a lunar eclipse

moon held in the afternoon sky.

Proposal

I'm not the man I used to be
        at times afraid

of what is going on outside—
        take for instance

this evening, another reading
        group of students, faculty

applause like slow persistent
        rainfall

slick avenue home
        like a child's racetrack

hang the blazer
        a chill lately

need Mr. Rogers' camel cardigan
        I should write you a letter

tell you this, we could work
        change your state.

Carnival

Funk, heavy bass
the Neville Brothers through speakers

hard back books on the shelf
a pile in progress, pages turned

down, there's a Celtic mist
and a harbinger, silver dollar

for better days ahead,
love letters to Heather

carnival rolls below
float procession, sack full of gold doubloons

pings the pavement, the flambeaux dip—
flame warns the kids

George Porter sings through floor length curtains
while I'm holding the coiled braid of Rapunzel.

Attic

Came early on my list to order and purge
two laptops from another century

and a working monitor—recycle at Best Buy.
Plastic bins with Christmas ornaments

and photo albums easy to stack on the right wall.
Some fifty stock wine glasses

black and white Rolling Stones posters—
Ebay candidates, along with framed floral prints.

But the dissertation notes wearing
leather cases, Iowa workshop folders

much less letters from Medbh in Belfast
and the collar from my first beagle. . .

at least there are two clear paths on the floorboards
along the heating units, a clean promise for spring.

Harry's Ace Hardware

Often two, three times a day
I shop there for free advice

at first, no list
just one item, a hose nozzle

then the entire hose, Nutri-Grow
fertilizer attachment…

there's a woman
wearing a brown bandana

buying air filters, a reminder
she hints at how handy I need to be—

Harry's swears a little W-D 40 goes a long way
like salt in the kitchen.

Fourteen aisles for the home
and garden is just enough,

flap for leaky toilet
copper key cut while you wait,

cast iron skillets, doorbells
and chandelier bulbs

stainless steel pots
weed killer and whacker—

wife expects the quick fix
I'm an apprentice
never can go to Lowes
just pop in, or Home Depot,

spend less than twenty bucks
and twenty minutes.

Dizzy Dean Baseball

I'm sitting in the aluminum stands
hoping James makes contact

before his third strike but he has not hit
this season so I'm told

four fathers coach
and pitch—its humid, steamy

grandparents under umbrellas
and this game runs by time on the scoreboard

my nephew in shades is an all star at second
and makes the important outs

into the double-header I'm a die-hard
on the edge of my hot seat

as James draws a long count
waits for a perfect pitch

from my brother-in law Freddie that he fouls
down third, I applaud, elated

as if a pop up is caught
or the rare fly over the fence.

My Maid Takes Her Shoes Off

barefoot on the hardwood floors
a faint slapping of distant waves

not like the staccato tick-tock
of my wife's heels on her way to work

she smokes on the back porch
sweeps, cleans the windows

she's so punctual that I never wonder
when she arrives each Tuesday.

We take and discuss inventory—
baby books on the nightstand

bottle of Mr. Clean half-empty
she has the code for the alarm

keys to our home
I pay her cash under a candle holder

while she mops her way out the front door.

Dawn Till Dusk

6:00 am—in our kitchen bay window
strands of Heather's golden hair in the light

she blends a fruit smoothie, walks the dogs
I am in the sea of dream

snoozing in our half-full cocoon,
my morning begs coffee—numbers crunched

in the home office—rosemary tamed in the garden,
brake tag grabbed for the car, I enjoy gym time

at dusk and this pulls up shades
on the evening, I can sense her

driving home, the wild
Atlantic salmon in tow.

Moment of Weakness

See you swallow
        my apology

taps the shoulder
        legs go—warm water washes over

your chignon undoes
        a meringue waterfall

lean-to we make during conversation
        when we're happy—

dogs blanket the hardwood
        floor in deep sleep

for purposeful silence—love something, someone
        quick—blow out

each candle before the flames
        dance in.

Divorcé, Dispirited

"She takes, she takes
and we are left with what
remains behind,"

my friend's father downed
another scotch on the second
floor of the Ritz Carlton

we proceeded to drink
on his tab after he turned in
our marriages went on

gorgeous wives in white
cackling on cream couches
over cocktails and jazz

flashing smiles, I slipped
out of conversation
for a moment, cornered

our minted graduate, as my wife
laughed out loud—the ballroom lights
laid its blanket for us

amidst midnight, swaying chandeliers
dangling diamond earrings
seersucker suits

our children tucked away—
we without one worry
despite the persistent rain outside.

Nursing

Colostrum begins at birth
skin to skin, her nipple

a swollen gumball
for our newborn

so I can't help
but watch, gaze

open mouthed as my son
fills and empties

his pea-sized stomach
every two hours

like an overcast sky
demands rain on sidewalks

she coaxes a good latch
while I hover

as her attention showers
like sunshine for our child

on the inclined hospital bed
her father looks away on the couch.

Newborn Son

> *See, I am sending an angel ahead of you*
> *to guard you along the way…*
>   —Exodus 23:20

Not that you need one
for your mother covers these southern shores

in case I slip, this card under
your door, Michael will do

especially in these infant, toddler years
though listen to your father

I'm geared for adolescence
and will tackle puberty, your teens…

always though there will be Michael
like music—that jazz through speakers

as school days offer Spring break
then summer breeze in early May—

largemouth bass lurk beneath
lily pads—alligators sun on the bank.

Toddler

There's this string
in my chest pulls me
back when I parent—
diapers, midnight cries,
need to be held, bouncing
baby greets the morning

and on this
sunny afternoon, early spring
you walk deliberately up
and down our street cackling
proud to reach another milestone…

could your mother and I care
too much?—I don't think so

seventeen months of joy, boy
oh boy can point out his nose,
shoulders, knees, and toes.

Avocado

There is very little to not like
at my favorite store they're never too ripe

nevertheless I feel the rind, pinch a little
they give like nipples

I put a firm one into my basket--
collage of salads, tortilla chips, chipotle

at home, my wife's hand
on the avocado skin, the seed

purple, hard as a rope's knot.

Monday

A wave of déjà vu as we cycle
the butterfly behind the zoo

it's the contrast of the freight liners
eye-level and baby-blue sky

my mind traces our path
this old mountain bike stuck

in gear and you riding so new
a champagne Townie with basket

all of the things we yet to fill
for a picnic—cheese, a pear

cool Chardonnay
wrapped with a tapestry for a blanket…

and I could not love the afternoon
with you any less

as the garage door smoothly opens
like a shade for the evening.

Other titles published recently by Five Oaks Press:

Karla Huston, *Grief Bone*
John Davis, Jr., *Hard Inheritance*
Sally Zakariya, *When You Escape*
Milton Bates, *Always on Fire*

www.ingramcontent.com/pod-product-compliance
Lightning Source LLC
Chambersburg PA
CBHW071748080526
44588CB00013B/2182